# Quick 'N' Easy
## Calendar Learning

Designer and illustrator: Christian H. Dutsch

Entire contents copyright © 1986 by David S. Lake Publishers, 19 Davis Drive, Belmont, California 94002. Permission is hereby granted to reproduce designated materials in this book for noncommercial and individual use.

ISBN–0–8224–5654–0

Printed in the United States of America

1. 9 8 7 6 5 4 3 2

Fearon Teacher Aids
a division of
**David S. Lake Publishers**
19 Davis Drive
Belmont, CA

# Teacher's Almanac

*Quick 'N' Easy Calendar Learning* is a unique collection of calendar-related activities for the entire school year. Each three-page section is completely reproducible and consists of a calendar to be filled in, a sticker page to be used with the calendar, and an activity page coordinated with one of the holidays or events in that month.

As they fill in the calendar pages, students will learn the names of the months, the number of days in each month, and the names and sequence of the days of the week. As they color, cut, and paste the stickers corresponding to each calendar page, they will learn about holidays whose dates are always the same, holidays whose dates change, the changes of seasons, special dates in history, and many other things. Stickers that remind students about school events will help them learn how to manage their time and plan ahead. "Remember to bring" stickers will help students develop a sense of responsibility and become more organized. Award stickers are included to give positive reinforcement for achievement in subject areas.

The following almanac contains information that will be useful with some of the stickers. Some references have been abbreviated, but they correspond clearly with the stickers.

## September

Balboa—25 (1513)
Citizenship Day—17 (anniversary of signing of Constitution, 1787)
First Day of Fall—22 or 23
Grandparents' Day—1st Sun. after Labor Day
Labor Day—1st Mon.
Mayflower Day—16 (departure from Plymouth, England, 1620)
Nat'l Good Neighbor Day—4th Sun.
Native American Day—4th Fri.

## October

Alfred Nobel's Birthday—21 (1833)
Columbus Day—12 (traditional); 2nd Mon. (observed)
John Lennon's Birthday—9 (1940)
Statue of Liberty—28 (1886)
Swallows leave—23
Thanksgiving (Canada)—2nd Mon.
United Nations Day—24
U.S. flag over Alaska—18 (1867)
World Poetry Day—15

## November

Dunce Day—8
Election Day—1st Tues. after 1st Mon.
Louisa May Alcott—29 (1832)
Marie Curie's Birthday—7 (1867)
Mickey Mouse—18 ("Steamboat Willie," 1928)
Mischief Night (Eng.)—4 (night before Guy Fawkes Day)
Remembrance Day (Canada)—11
Sesame Street begins—10 (1969)
Thanksgiving (U.S.)—usually 4th Thurs.
Veterans Day (U.S.)—11

## December

Beethoven's Birthday—16 (1770)
Bill of Rights Day—15
Boston Tea Party—16 (1773)
1st Day of Winter—21 or 22
Human Rights Day—10
Pearl Harbor Day—7 (1941)
*Poor Richard's Almanac*—19 (1732)
Wright Brothers—17 (Kitty Hawk, N.C., 1903)

## January

Elvis Presley—8 (1935)
Gold in California—24 (1848)
Martin Luther King—15 (1929)
Mozart's Birthday—27 (1756)
Nat'l Handwriting Day—23
Nat'l Nothing Day—16
Trivia Day—4
World Literacy Day—8

## February

Babe Ruth—6 (1895)
Boy Scouts founded—8 (1910)
Groundhog Day—2
Midwinter Day—6
Nat'l Inventors' Day—11
Presidents' Day—3rd Mon.
Robinson Crusoe Day—1 (a 1709 rescue inspires Defoe)
Thomas Edison—11 (1847)

## March

Agriculture Day—24
Buzzards return—15
Coca-Cola® invented—29 (1886)
1st Day of Spring—20 or 21
1st Space Walk—18 (1965)
Girl Scouts founded—12 (1912)
Johnny Appleseed Day—11
Nellie Melba—23 (1901)
Swallows return—19

## April

Arbor Day—often on last Fri.
Booker T. Washington—5? (1856)
John Muir—21 (1838)
Paul Revere's Ride—18 (1775)
Walpurgis Night—30 (eve of May Day—witches ride)
World Health Day—7

## May

Armed Forces Day—3rd Sat.
Cinco de Mayo—5
John F. Kennedy—29 (1917)
May Day—1
Memorial Day—usually last Mon.
Mother's Day—2nd Sun.
Mt. St. Helens—18 (1980)
Victoria Day—1st Mon. before 25
World Red Cross Day—8

## June

D-Day—6 (1944)
Father's Day—3rd Sun.
1st Day of Summer—20 or 21
Flag Day—14 (1777)
Magna Carta—15 (1215)
Midsummer Day—24 (birthday of John the Baptist)
Teacher's Day—Thurs. before Memorial Day
World Environment Day—5

Name _____

# September 19__

| Sun. | Mon. | Tues. | Wed. | Thurs. | Fri. | Sat. |
|------|------|-------|------|--------|------|------|
| —    | —    | —     | —    | —      | —    | —    |
| —    | —    | —     | —    | —      | —    | —    |
| —    | —    | —     | —    | —      | —    | —    |
| —    | —    | —     | —    | —      | —    | —    |
| —    | —    | —     |      |        |      |      |

*Quick 'N' Easy Calendar Learning*, copyright © 1986 David S. Lake Publishers

Name _____

# September Stickers

| | | | | | | |
|---|---|---|---|---|---|---|
| Labor Day | 1st Day of Fall | Native American Day | Grandparents' Day | Balboa discovers Pacific Ocean | Citizenship Day | Mayflower Day |
| School Starts | Good Neighbor Day | Sports | Birthday | Birthday | School Trip | Remember to bring |
| No School | Class Party | Good Work in Language | Birthday | Birthday | School Trip | Remember to bring |
| No School | Class Party | Good Work in Math | Good Work in Reading | Good Work in Spelling | Sports | Remember to bring |

## Use the spaces below to design your own stickers.

Quick 'N' Easy Calendar Learning, copyright © 1986 David S. Lake Publishers

## September

# Classroom Map

In the space below, draw a map of your classroom. Show the desks, chairs, chalkboard, flag, door, windows, clock, pencil sharpener, and wastepaper basket. Use the key or make up one of your own.

**Key**

| | | | | | |
|---|---|---|---|---|---|
| chair | ◯ | door | ⊣\⊨ | clock | 🕐 |
| chalkboard | ▭ | desk | ▱ | window | ⊣—⊨ |
| wastepaper basket | ⊔ | flag | 🏴 | pencil sharpener | ✐ |

Quick 'N' Easy Calendar Learning, copyright © 1986 David S. Lake Publishers

Name _____

# October 19__

| Sun. | Mon. | Tues. | Wed. | Thurs. | Fri. | Sat. |
|------|------|-------|------|--------|------|------|
| — | — | — | — | — | — | — |
| — | — | — | — | — | — | — |
| — | — | — | — | — | — | — |
| — | — | — | — | — | — | — |
| — | — | — | | | | |

Quick 'N' Easy Calendar Learning, copyright © 1986 David S. Lake Publishers

Name _____

# October Stickers

| | | | | | | |
|---|---|---|---|---|---|---|
| Columbus Day | Halloween | Thanksgiving (Canada) | Swallows leave San Juan Capistrano | United Nations Day | World Poetry Day | John Lennon's Birthday |
| U. S. flag raised over Alaska | Statue of Liberty dedicated | Alfred Nobel's Birthday | No School | Sports | School Trip | Remember to bring |
| Class Party | Good Work | Birthday | Birthday | Birthday | School Trip | Remember to bring |
| Class Party | Good Work in Reading | Good Work in Language | Good Work in Math | Birthday | Sports | Remember to bring |

## Use the spaces below to design your own stickers.

Quick 'N' Easy Calendar Learning, copyright © 1986 David S. Lake Publishers

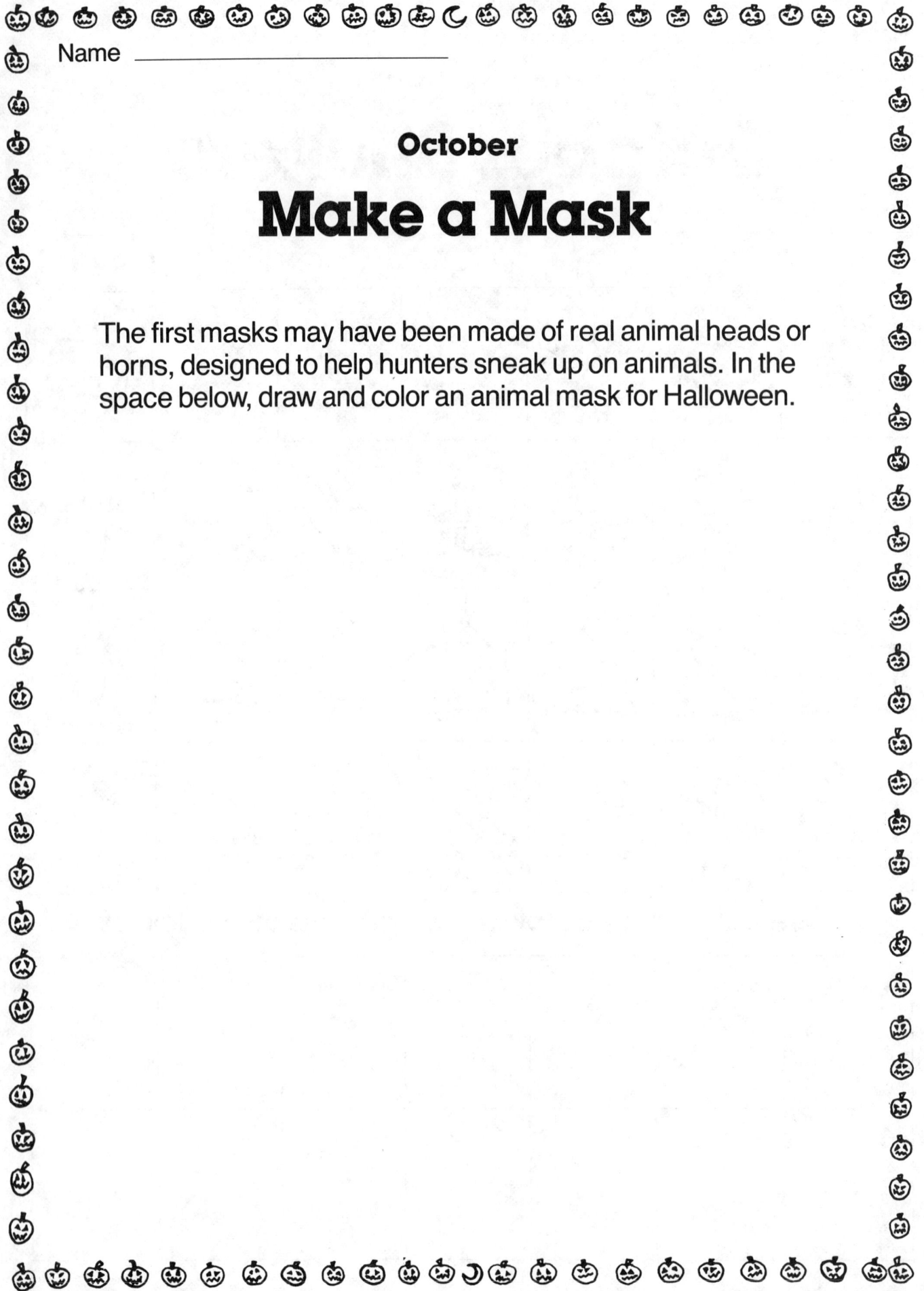

Name _____

# Make a Mask

The first masks may have been made of real animal heads or horns, designed to help hunters sneak up on animals. In the space below, draw and color an animal mask for Halloween.

*Quick 'N' Easy Calendar Learning*, copyright © 1986 David S. Lake Publishers

Name _____

# November 19__

| Sun. | Mon. | Tues. | Wed. | Thurs. | Fri. | Sat. |
|------|------|-------|------|--------|------|------|
| — | — | — | — | — | — | — |
| — | — | — | — | — | — | — |
| — | — | — | — | — | — | — |
| — | — | — | — | — | — | — |
| — | — | — | | | | |

Quick 'N' Easy Calendar Learning, copyright © 1986 David S. Lake Publishers

Name _____

# November Stickers

| | | | | | | |
|---|---|---|---|---|---|---|
| Thanksgiving U. S. | Election Day | Veterans Day | Remembrance Day (Canada) | Mischief Night (England) | Dunce Day | Marie Curie's Birthday |
| Louisa May Alcott's Birthday | Sesame Street begins | No School | No School | Class Party | Class Party | Remember to bring |
| Mickey Mouse's first cartoon | Good Work in Reading | Good Work in Math | Birthday | Birthday | School Trip | Remember to bring |
| Sports | Good Work in Language | Good Work | Birthday | Birthday | School Trip | Remember to bring |

## Use the spaces below to design your own stickers.

Quick 'N' Easy Calendar Learning, copyright © 1986 David S. Lake Publishers

Name _____

## November

# Thanksgiving Feast

What do you eat on Thanksgiving Day? Many countries celebrate a day of thanksgiving. Choose a country and find out what foods are eaten on its day of thanksgiving. Then, fill in the menu.

## Menu

Country:

Appetizer:

Main dish:

Side dishes:

Desserts:

Drinks:

Quick 'N' Easy Calendar Learning, copyright © 1986 David S. Lake Publishers

# December 19__

| Sun. | Mon. | Tues. | Wed. | Thurs. | Fri. | Sat. |
|------|------|-------|------|--------|------|------|
| — | — | — | — | — | — | — |
| — | — | — | — | — | — | — |
| — | — | — | — | — | — | — |
| — | — | — | — | — | — | — |
| — | — | — | | | | |

Quick 'N' Easy Calendar Learning, copyright © 1986 David S. Lake Publishers

Name _____

# December Stickers

| | | | | | | |
|---|---|---|---|---|---|---|
| 1st Day of Winter | Pearl Harbor Day | Human Rights Day | Christmas Day | Hanukkah celebration begins | Bill of Rights Day | Wright Brothers' 1st Flight |
| Boston Tea Party | Beethoven's Birthday | Sports | Sports | Birthday | | Remember to bring |
| No School | Poor Richard's Almanac published | School Trip | School Trip | Birthday | Birthday | Remember to bring |
| No School | Class Party | Good Work in Reading | Good Work in Language | Good Work | Birthday | Remember to bring |

## Use the spaces below to design your own stickers.

Quick 'N' Easy Calendar Learning, copyright © 1986 David S. Lake Publishers

11

**December**

# All-Purpose Gift List

'Tis the season for gift-giving. Use the spaces below to make your shopping list. Put a check in the blank beside each name after you buy or make the gift.

**Name**                    **Gift**

Quick 'N' Easy Calendar Learning, copyright © 1986 David S. Lake Publishers

Quick 'N' Easy Calendar Learning, copyright © 1986 Davic S. Lake Publishers

Name _____

# January 19__

| Sun. | Mon. | Tues. | Wed. | Thurs. | Fri. | Sat. |
|------|------|-------|------|--------|------|------|
| — | — | — | — | — | — | — |
| — | — | — | — | — | — | — |
| — | — | — | — | — | — | — |
| — | — | — | — | — | — | — |
| — | — | — | | | | |

Name _____

# January Stickers

| | | | | | | |
|---|---|---|---|---|---|---|
| New Year's Day | World Literacy Day | Elvis Presley's Birthday | Martin Luther King's Birthday | Gold discovered in California | National Handwriting Day | Trivia Day |
| National Nothing Day | Mozart's Birthday | Weather Report | Sports | Good Work in Spelling | Good Work in Reading | Remember to bring |
| Good Work in Math | No School | Class Party | Birthday | Birthday | School Trip | Remember to bring |
| Good Work | No School | Class Party | Birthday | Birthday | School Trip | Remember to bring |

## Use the spaces below to design your own stickers.

Quick 'N' Easy Calendar Learning, copyright © 1986 David S. Lake Publishers

14

### January

# Make a Banner

World Literacy Day is in January. Choose a book from the library and read it. Use the banner pattern below to tell about your book. Cut out your banner and display it. Use the other pattern to make a bookmark for the books you will read this year.

Title: _____
Author: _____
Book reviewer: _____
Date: _____

This book belongs to _____

Quick 'N' Easy Calendar Learning, copyright © 1986 David S. Lake Publishers

Name _____

# February 19__

| Sun. | Mon. | Tues. | Wed. | Thurs. | Fri. | Sat. |
|------|------|-------|------|--------|------|------|
| __ | __ | __ | __ | __ | __ | __ |
| __ | __ | __ | __ | __ | __ | __ |
| __ | __ | __ | __ | __ | __ | __ |
| __ | __ | __ | __ | __ | __ | __ |
| __ | __ | __ | | | | |

Quick 'N' Easy Calendar Learning, copyright © 1986 David S. Lake Publishers

Name _____

# February Stickers

| | | | | | | |
|---|---|---|---|---|---|---|
| Valentine's Day | Groundhog Day | Robinson Crusoe Day | Leap Year Day | National Inventors' Day | Thomas Edison's Birthday | Boy Scouts founded |
| Babe Ruth's Birthday | Presidents' Day | Midwinter Day | Sports | Birthday | Birthday | Remember to bring |
| No School | Class Party | Good Work in Reading | Good Work in Language | Birthday | Birthday | Remember to bring |
| No School | Class Party | Good Work in Math | Good Work in Spelling | School Trip | School Trip | Remember to bring |

## Use the spaces below to design your own stickers.

Quick 'N' Easy Calendar Learning, copyright © 1986 David S. Lake Publishers

## February

# Make a Weather Chart

Keep a record of the weather in the spaces below. Just before you leave school each afternoon, fill in the chart. Use a symbol from the key to illustrate each day's weather.

**Key**

cold   windy   rain   snow   hail   frost

sunny   warm   fog   thunderstorm   cloudy   hot

| Mon. | Tues. | Wed. | Thurs. | Fri. |
|------|-------|------|--------|------|
|      |       |      |        |      |
|      |       |      |        |      |
|      |       |      |        |      |
|      |       |      |        |      |
|      |       |      |        |      |

Quick 'N' Easy Calendar Learning, copyright © 1986 David S. Lake Publishers

Name _____

# March 19__

| Sun. | Mon. | Tues. | Wed. | Thurs. | Fri. | Sat. |
|------|------|-------|------|--------|------|------|
| — | — | — | — | — | — | — |
| — | — | — | — | — | — | — |
| — | — | — | — | — | — | — |
| — | — | — | — | — | — | — |
| — | — | — | | | | |

Quick 'N' Easy Calendar Learning, copyright © 1986 David S. Lake Publishers

# March Stickers

| | | | | | | |
|---|---|---|---|---|---|---|
| 1st Day of Spring | Johnny Appleseed Day | St. Patrick's Day | Nellie Melba first made toast | Agriculture Day | Girl Scouts founded | 1st Space Walk |
| Buzzards return to Hinckley, Ohio | Coca-Cola® invented | Swallows return to San Juan Capistrano | Birthday | Birthday | Class Party | Remember to bring |
| No School | School Trip | School Trip | Birthday | Birthday | Class Party | Remember to bring |
| Sports | Sports | Good Work | Good Work in Reading | Good Work in Spelling | Good Work in Language | Remember to bring |

## Use the spaces below to design your own stickers.

Quick 'N' Easy Calendar Learning, copyright © 1986 David S. Lake Publishers

## March

# Graph the Degrees

Color the bars in the graphs below to show each day's highest temperature. Over the four weeks shown in your graph, do the temperatures get warmer? colder? _____

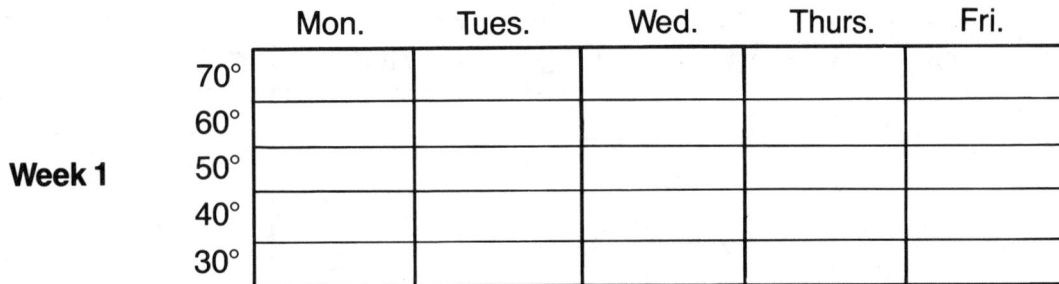

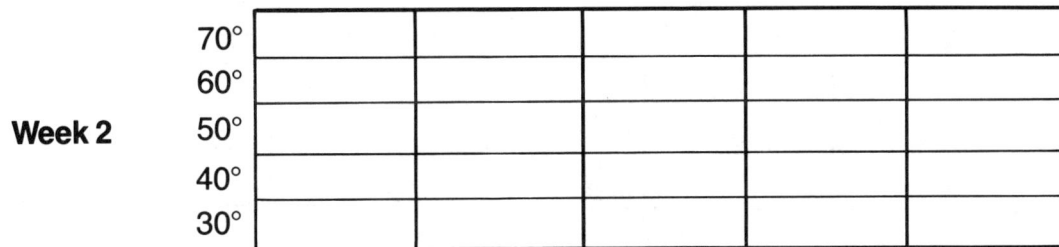

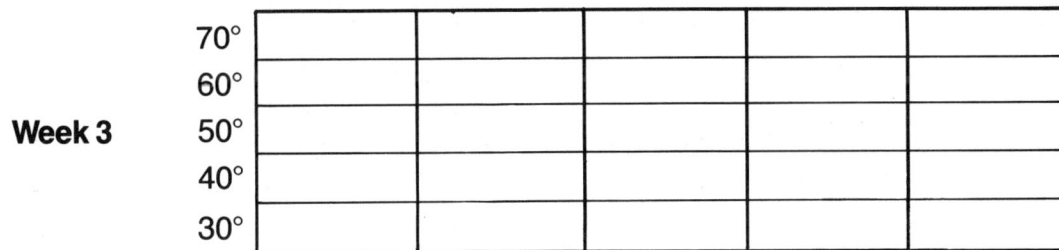

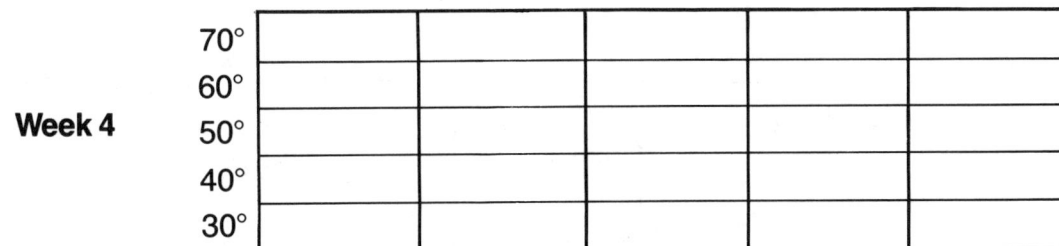

|  | Mon. | Tues. | Wed. | Thurs. | Fri. |
|---|---|---|---|---|---|

**Week 1**
70°
60°
50°
40°
30°

**Week 2**
70°
60°
50°
40°
30°

**Week 3**
70°
60°
50°
40°
30°

**Week 4**
70°
60°
50°
40°
30°

Quick 'N' Easy Calendar Learning, copyright © 1986 David S. Lake Publishers

Name _____

# April 19__

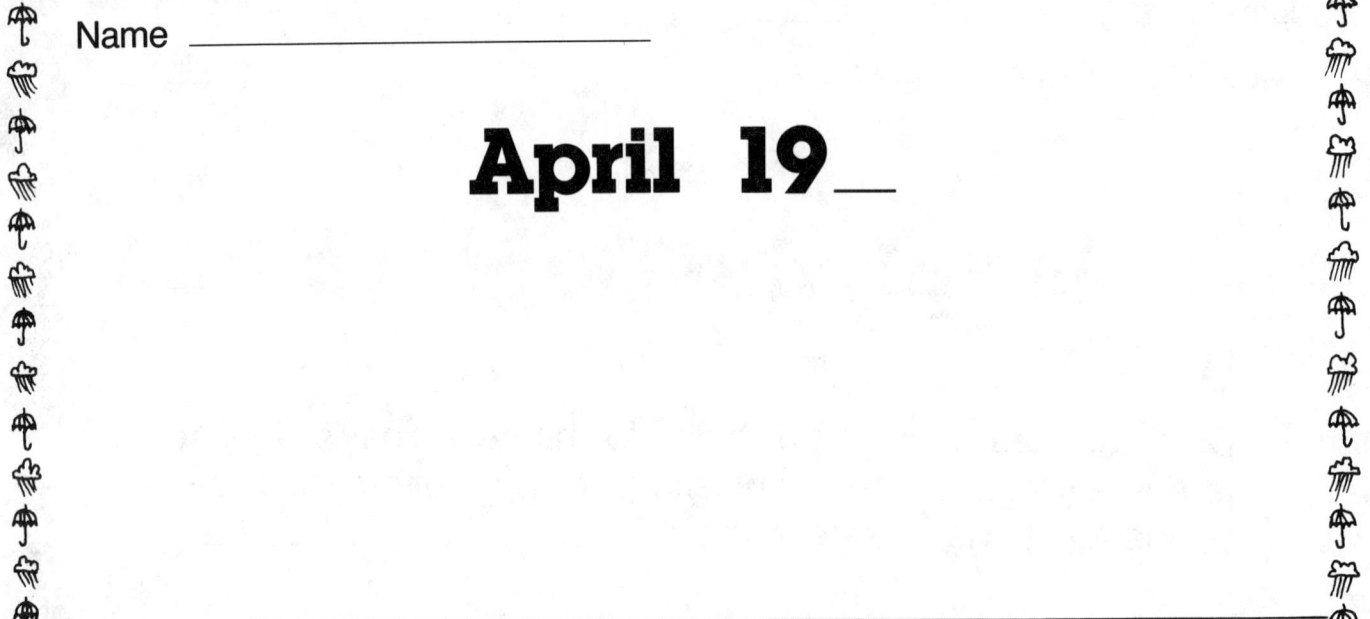

| Sun. | Mon. | Tues. | Wed. | Thurs. | Fri. | Sat. |
|------|------|-------|------|--------|------|------|
| — | — | — | — | — | — | — |
| — | — | — | — | — | — | — |
| — | — | — | — | — | — | — |
| — | — | — | — | — | — | — |
| — | — | — | | | | |

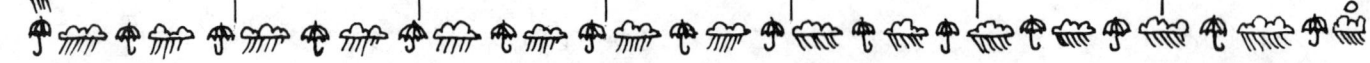

Quick 'N' Easy Calendar Learning, copyright © 1986 David S. Lake Publishers

22

Name _____

# April Stickers

| | | | | | | |
|---|---|---|---|---|---|---|
| April Fools' Day | World Health Day | Arbor Day | Walpurgis Night | Easter (most of the time) | Paul Revere's Midnight Ride | Passover (most of the time) |
| Taxes due | John Muir's Birthday | Booker T. Washington's Birthday | Sports | Birthday | Birthday | School Trip |
| Remember to bring | No School | No School | Class Party | Good Work in Reading | Good Work in Language | School Trip |
| Remember to bring | Remember to bring | Birthday | Class Party | Good Work in Math | Sports | Birthday |

## Use the spaces below to design your own stickers.

*Quick 'N' Easy Calendar Learning,* copyright © 1986 David S. Lake Publishers

**April**

# Science Scavenger

National Arbor Day is observed in April. *Arbor* comes from the Latin word for tree, and an *aboretum* is a collection of many trees. Make your own arboretum by collecting leaves to match the drawings in the boxes below. Paste your leaves in the blank boxes.

| | | |
|---|---|---|
| toothed | simple | lobed |
| toothed | simple | lobed |

*Quick 'N' Easy Calendar Learning,* copyright © 1986 David S. Lake Publishers

# May 19__

| Sun. | Mon. | Tues. | Wed. | Thurs. | Fri. | Sat. |
|------|------|-------|------|--------|------|------|
| — | — | — | — | — | — | — |
| — | — | — | — | — | — | — |
| — | — | — | — | — | — | — |
| — | — | — | — | — | — | — |
| — | — | — | | | | |

*Quick 'N' Easy Calendar Learning,* copyright © 1986 David S. Lake Publishers

Name _____

# May Stickers

| | | | | | | |
|---|---|---|---|---|---|---|
| May Day | Cinco de Mayo | John F. Kennedy's Birthday | Memorial Day | Mother's Day | Victoria Day (Canada) | Armed Forces Day |
| World Red Cross Day | Mt. St. Helens erupted | Weather Report | Birthday | Birthday | School Trip | Remember to bring |
| No School | Class Party | Good Work | Birthday | Birthday | School Trip | Remember to bring |
| No School | Class Party | Good Work in Spelling | Good Work in Reading | Good Work in Language | Sports | Remember to bring |

## Use the spaces below to design your own stickers.

*Quick 'N' Easy Calendar Learning*, copyright © 1986 David S. Lake Publishers

**May**

# Think, Draw, and Write

Fill this piñata with surprises. Then write a story about breaking open the piñata.

_____
_____
_____
_____
_____
_____
_____
_____

Use the other side.

Quick 'N' Easy Calendar Learning, copyright © 1986 David S. Lake Publishers

Name _____

# June 19__

| Sun. | Mon. | Tues. | Wed. | Thurs. | Fri. | Sat. |
|------|------|-------|------|--------|------|------|
| — | — | — | — | — | — | — |
| — | — | — | — | — | — | — |
| — | — | — | — | — | — | — |
| — | — | — | — | — | — | — |
| — | — | — | | | | |

Quick 'N' Easy Calendar Learning, copyright © 1986 David S. Lake Publishers

Name _____

# June Stickers

| | | | | | | |
|---|---|---|---|---|---|---|
| Flag Day | Father's Day | 1st Day of Summer | Last Day of School | World Environment Day | Teacher's Day | D-Day |
| Magna Carta signed | Midsummer Day | Sports | Birthday | Birthday | School Trip | Remember to bring |
| No School | Class Party | | Birthday | Birthday | School Trip | Remember to bring |
| No School | Class Party | Good Work in Reading | Good Work in Language | Good Work | Sports | Remember to bring |

## Use the spaces below to design your own stickers.

Quick 'N' Easy Calendar Learning, copyright © 1986 David S. Lake Publishers

## June

# Design a Flag

June 14 is Flag Day. Flags tell something about a country or a kingdom. Use the space below to draw and color a flag that tells something about you. Think about including your name, pets, or favorite foods or television shows on your special flag.

Quick 'N' Easy Calendar Learning, copyright © 1986 David S. Lake Publishers